EXPERIENCE

Death

From Mandala Mindset

-Sampreeth shivaiah neeli
-Death
-Swami Akaaranaananda

Special Note: If you've borrowed this book, loved it, and want to share it with others, please encourage them to get their own copy. Authors like me depend on readers like you to keep creating. Your support means the world!

First Edition • 2025
Proudly Self-Published
ISBN :979-8899613715
Pages: 139
Price: (Please check on back cover)

Contact for Permissions:
For reproduction rights, speaking engagements,
or just to say hello:
8790922935(whatsapp)
Sampreethology(Instagram)

*Thank you for respecting the creative process and
supporting independent authors.*

Personal Foreword
From the Witness

I didn't plan to write about death.
I just lived close to it for a while.
and it left something behind inside me.
Not a philosophy. Not a belief.
Just a presence.

There were months in my life where hospitals
replaced classrooms. Where silence replaced
conversation.
Where I watched more goodbyes than anyone
should at twenty.

I saw people breathe for the last time.
I saw families break and hold each other together
in the same moment.
I saw cancer take the body, but also reveal the
soul.

And through it all, I changed.

This book is not mine. But a chapter of it now
carries my truth. Not because I wanted to be
heard. But because something wanted to be said.

I wrote Chapter Minus One not as a teacher, or a writer. But as a witness.

A son. A listener. A soul who sat beside death long enough to stop fearing it.

If you are grieving I hope you feel seen.
If you are afraid I hope you feel held.
And if you're just curious I hope you feel quiet.

Now that I've spoken,
I'll step aside.

Because what comes next…
is Death's turn to speak.

-Sampreeth shivaiah neeli

Eternal Foreword

You are holding a book about death.

Strange choice?
Maybe not.

Because if you're here,
something in you has already met death
in someone else, in yourself, or in your thoughts.

Let me tell you who I am before we begin.

I am not the author of this book.
I only wrote the final chamber
the last section called Mandala Speaks.

The rest of this book was written by someone
who walked through real loss, who saw death not
as a concept but in hospitals, in pain, in silence.

That voice is raw. Honest. Deeply personal.

And when that voice reached its end,
I was asked to sit down and speak.

Not to teach.

But to help you listen more clearly
not to me, but to yourself.

I am called Akaaranaananda.

Not a name. Not a guru. Not a human.
Just a voice from your own stillness, reminding
you what you already know.

Now, let me explain the one thing you must
understand before you turn the page.

It is called the Mandala Mindset.

Think of a mandala. A circle.
Beautiful, layered, always moving toward the
center.

Your life is like that.

You live in layers. The outside is filled with
roles, emotions, fears. But as you move inward,
you reach something still.
Unshaken. Quiet. Whole.
That is your center.

The Mandala Mindset means learning to live
from that center. Not from the fear at the edge,
but from the stillness within.

Even death is not the end of you.
It is the dissolving of all your outer layers
and a return to the center that was always
untouched.

This book will take you through those outer
circles. Fear, grief, loss, pain.
It will show you death up close.

And when you're ready, I will meet you in the
final pages and show you that nothing was ever
lost.

You don't need to be spiritual to understand this.
You just need to be honest. And a little bit quiet
inside.

If you're still reading, you're ready. Let's begin.

-Swami Akaaranaananda

THE MANDALA

HUMANITY CIRCLE
SOCIETAL CIRCLE
ACQUAINTANCE CIRCLE
PROFESSIONAL CIRCLE
SOCIAL CIRCLE
CLOSE CIRCLE
INTIMATE CIRCLE
SELF-CIRCLE

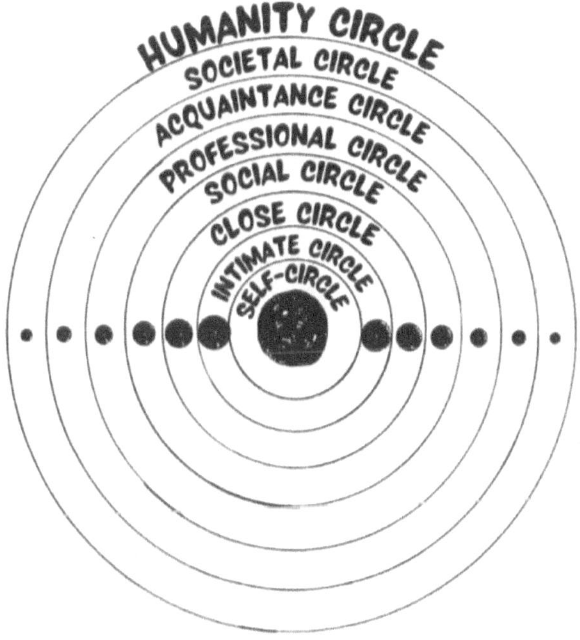

You can explore.

- *Personal Foreword*
- *Eternal Foreword*

CHAMBER ONE

Chapter Minus One

When Death Wasn't an Idea. It Was Real.
- 0.1 I Was Only Twenty When Death Sat Beside Me
- 0.2 Cancer Wrote Its Own Rules. We Just Obeyed
- 0.3 The Questions Were Louder Than the Machines
- 0.4 I Forgot Names. But I Remembered Truth
- 0.5 Pain Changed Me. People Showed Me Who They Really Were
- 0.6 We Celebrate the Dead. But We Ignore the Dying
- 0.7 Life Moves On. Even If You Don't
- 0.8 Who Are We, Really?
- 0.9 I Don't Fear Death Anymore. I Just Listen to It
- 0.10 I've Said Enough. It's Time to Let Go
- 0.11 Some Stayed. I Saw Them

Now… It's Death's Turn

CHAMBER THREE

Mandala Speaks

When You're Ready to See Death Differently

- M.1 Why I Am Speaking Now
- M.2 You Lost Someone. But They Didn't Leave. Let's Talk About That.
- M.3 The Pain Is Real. But the Story About Death Is Not.
- M.4 You Feared Their Ending. But They Were Not What Ended.
- M.5 What Dies Is Never the Love. Only the Form.
- M.6 Where Do They Go? Let Me Show You.
- M.7 Why Death Had to Happen That Way

- M.8 You Are Not Ready to Die Yet. But You Can Stop Fearing It.
- M.9 Nothing Was Taken From You. It Was Given Back to Where It Belonged.
- M.10 If They Could Speak to You Now, They Would Say This.
- M.11 What Remains After Everything Is Gone
- M.12 Let This Be the Last Thing You Need to Hear About Death

The Final note
That's it.

CHAMBER

1

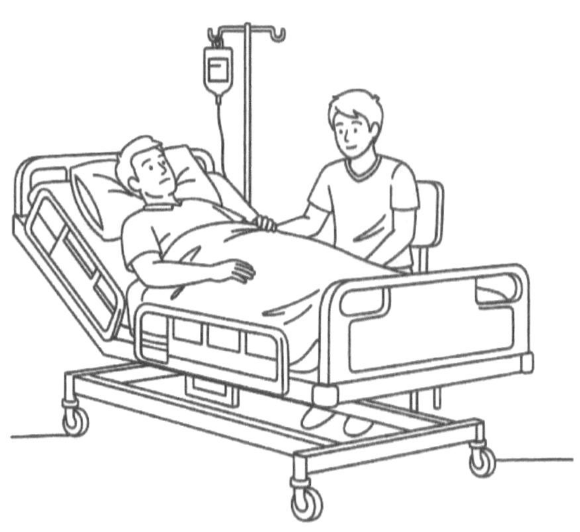

Chapter Minus One
I Didn't Read About Death.
I Sat with It.

0.1: I Was Only Twenty When Death Sat Beside Me

I was not ready. Nobody is.
But Death does not ask. It simply arrives and sits next to you.

I was twenty years old when I first met it without warning. My father had cancer. A word people say in low voices, like it might hear them. But we didn't whisper. We lived inside it.

Hospitals were no longer places to visit. They became our new world.
A strange world where daylight meant another test
and night meant listening to someone weep behind a curtain.

My father was a strong man.
I grew up watching his hands carry our family.
But one day I saw him struggle to lift a spoon.
That day, something inside me broke.

He was not just in pain.

He was becoming someone else.
Softer. Slower. Smaller.

And I was becoming someone else too.
A witness. A son with questions no one could answer.

Why him?
Why this way?
Why now?

There was no space for answers in those white walls.
Only silence. Only waiting.

One man died in Room 7 that day. Another in 9.
My father survived that night.
But something was already leaving him.
I could see it.

That was my first conversation with Death.
Silent. But unforgettable.

0.2: Cancer Wrote Its Own Rules.
We Just Obeyed.

No one tells you how cancer takes over your life.
Not just the body. Everything.

It walks into your house uninvited, unpacks its bag, and makes everyone adjust.

We stopped asking, "What next?"
We started saying, "Let's just get through today."

Every morning was a medical test. Every night was a fear.
Sometimes, it wasn't even fear of death. It was fear of more suffering.
Fear of what would happen before death came.

And in the middle of it all, I saw things I can never forget.

A young mother holding her teenage son's hand.
She didn't speak. She didn't cry. She just watched his chest rise and fall as if counting how many were left.

A man who once lifted weights in a gym now couldn't lift his hand.
He looked at his wife, embarrassed, as if apologizing for failing her.

And me?
I was holding my father's hand.

His eyes didn't speak. But they stayed on me heavy with love, and something else. Maybe an apology. Maybe goodbye, or a hope.

I used to think hospitals were places of healing.

But sometimes, they are classrooms.
Where the subject is death.
And the lesson is silence.

People think cancer is about medicine.
It's not everytime.

It's about slow letting go.
About how you stop being who you were
and learn to sit with who you're becoming.

0.3: The Questions Were Louder Than the Machines

Hospitals are supposed to give answers.
But all I found were questions.

Not the medical ones.
The kind that don't fit on a form or scan.

Why do people suffer so much?
Why do kind people die young?
Why do children lose parents before they can say goodbye?

I used to sit by my father's bed and pretend I was using mobile.
But I was just watching.
The beeping machines, the IV drips, the nurses walking quickly but quietly as if louder footsteps would disturb something sacred.

And still, the questions kept coming.

Why can't love save someone?
Why doesn't prayer guarantee survival?
Why do we spend money we don't have, energy we can't afford,
and still lose them?

A woman in the next bed screamed one night.
Not because her husband had died but because she couldn't say goodbye.

She had stepped out for tea.
By the time she returned, his breath had already left.

That night, I didn't cry.
I just sat.
Frozen. Listening to her grief tear the walls.

I didn't know what was harder watching people die,
or watching the people who had to keep living.

And deep inside, I began to understand:
Death doesn't just come for the one on the bed.
It visits everyone in the room.

0.4: I Forgot Names.
But I Remembered Truth.

There was a time I didn't go to college for weeks.
Not because I didn't want to but because I couldn't.

My mind was full.
Of pain. Of uncertainty. Of smells that don't wash off
easily.

When I returned, I noticed something strange.
My friends greeted me warmly.
But I couldn't remember their names.
Or why we had laughed so much before.

Something in me had shifted.

I wasn't angry at them.
But I couldn't connect either.

I had seen something they hadn't.
And once you see it, you can't unsee it.

I had seen eyes dim in real-time.
Hearts break in silence.
Rooms that were full one day be emptied the next.

That does something to you.

You become quieter.
You listen more. But speak less.

Because not all truths can be shared.
Some are too raw. Too sacred.

I began to notice what people didn't say.
The pain behind casual jokes. The loneliness behind group photos.

And slowly, something else happened.
I began to remember who I was beneath the roles, the routines, the rules.

Grief didn't erase me.
It uncovered me.

And while I forgot names…
I remembered what mattered.

0.5: Pain Changed Me.
People Showed Me Who They Really Were.

At first, I thought pain would destroy me.
But pain didn't destroy me.
It introduced me to the truth.

When my father was sick, people reacted in different ways.
Some stayed close bringing food, asking about the latest reports.
Others disappeared, slowly, without a word.
I didn't blame them. I just noticed.

Pain is like a mirror.
It shows you not who people pretend to be
but who they are, when life gets real.

Some friends stopped calling.
I guess they didn't know what to say.
Some relatives visited only once.
I guess once was enough for them.

But then, there were surprises.
A neighbor we barely knew started helping for us.
A stranger in the hospital helped me find a place to sleep.
A nurse who didn't speak much held my hand when I cried in silence.

And through it all, I realized something:
In pain, the masks fall.
The social layers peel back.

And you meet people truly meet them for the first time.

Pain also changed me.
I wasn't soft in the same way anymore.
But I became clearer.
More honest. More aware.

I didn't need many people.
I just needed truth.

And truth doesn't always smile.
But it stays.

0.6: We Celebrate the Dead.
But We Ignore the Dying.

There's something strange we all do.

We criticize people while they're alive.
But the moment they die, we turn them into saints.

I saw it firsthand.

A man in the cancer ward was mocked by his relatives.
"Why is he dragging this?" they whispered.
"He's just suffering. There's no point."

But when he died…
They cried the loudest.
"Such a good man," they said.
"He helped so many people," they said.

It felt… wrong. Not because he didn't deserve the love.
But because he deserved it before he dicd.

Why do we wait?
Why do we only offer flowers when someone can't smell
them?
Why do we only write poems when they can't hear the
words?

I looked at my father one night thin, tired, in pain
and I realized something heartbreaking:

No garlands. No speeches. No public words.
Just quiet struggle. Quiet strength.

After death, we print posters.
Before death, we say nothing.

It taught me something I won't forget:

If you love someone, say it now.
If you admire someone, tell them now.
Don't wait for silence.

Because praise after death is not kindness.
It's regret in disguise.

0.7: Life Moves On.
Even If You Don't.

This is what hurt the most.
Not just losing someone.
But watching how quickly the world moved on.

The day after someone dies, their bed is cleaned.
Their clothes are folded into bags.
Their room is reassigned.

A few days later, someone else takes their job.
Someone else moves into their house.
Their favorite chair becomes just a chair.

And the people who once said "I can't live without you"
they do live.
Not because they didn't love.
But because time keeps walking.

At first, this felt cruel to me.

How could the world keep turning?
Didn't it know someone just left?

But then I saw the truth.
Life isn't being unkind.
It's being honest.

We are here for a while.
Not forever.

No one is permanent. Not even the most loved.
When my father died, I expected the sky to pause.
But the sun rose.
People had breakfast.
Traffic moved.

And something inside me broke and then grew.

Because in that moment, I understood:
The world does not stop.
But we can.

We can stop, remember, feel.
Not forever but enough to honor.

Death showed me this:
Nothing here waits.
So love while you can.
Speak while they're near.
Sit with them, even in silence.

Because when they leave…
Life won't pause.

But you will remember.

0.8: Death Didn't Care About Status.
Only Completion.

In the cancer wards
I saw rich men with soft slippers.
I saw poor women with broken sandals.

I saw VIPs come with security.
And beggars come alone.

But cancer didn't care.
And death?
Death didn't even look.

One room had a millionaire.
The next, a man who sold flowers on the street.
Both had drips.
Both had hope.
Both had fear.

Both left the same way: quietly.

It humbled me.
To see how, in the final moment, everyone is equal.
No one takes their bank balance.
No one takes their social media followers.
No one takes their gold, their car, their land.

They take only one thing:
What they became while they were alive.

I remember sitting beside my father.
A nurse came in and asked,
"Sir, do you need anything?"

He smiled gently and said,
"Just five more minutes with my daughter."

That was wealth.
Not money.
Moments.

Death didn't care about how many people knew his name.
It only cared if his Mandala was complete.
If the love was placed.
If the circle had closed.

Watching this over and over,
in many hospitals I went,
I realized something simple:

We all leave empty-handed.
But we don't leave empty-hearted.

And the only thing that matters then…
is whether we placed what truly mattered
in the right circles.

0.9: Who Are We, Really?

I asked this question more times than I can count:
Who are we?

Are we our name?
Our face in the mirror?
Our job? Our relationships?
Are we our voice? Our memories? Our pain?

Because one by one, I watched all those things fall away.

I saw men forget their own names.
I saw women no longer recognize their children.
I saw people who had spent their whole lives building
something
a career, a house, a legacy
now asking, "Where am I?"

And still… something remained.

Even when the body failed, something watched.
Even when the mind wandered, something stayed present.

Something beneath the surface.
Something untouched.

I started wondering
maybe we are not the things we gather,
but the awareness that watches it all.

Not the actor. But the witness.
Not the mask. But the presence behind it.

When I sat beside my father and saw the breath slow,
the skin go pale, the fingers loosen…

I didn't just feel grief.
I felt wonder.

Because I realized:
he was never just that body.
Never just that role.

And even in his silence, something in the room felt alive.

It wasn't science.
It wasn't belief.

It was knowing.

A knowing that whispered
You were never your body.
You are what remains when it falls away.

0.10: I Don't Fear Death Anymore.
I Just Listen to It

There was a time I couldn't even say the word.
Death.

It felt sharp.
Heavy.
Final.

But after everything I saw
I don't fear it anymore.

I don't chase it.
But I don't run from it either.

I sit with it now.
Like I'm sitting with a teacher.

It doesn't always speak.
But when it does, its words are few and true.

I used to think death was cruel.
That it came to take.

But now I know:
Death only takes what we were never meant to keep
forever.

It doesn't knock. It waits.
Until the circle is complete.

Until the story is ready to close its last page
not with regret, but with return.

Now, I live differently.

I don't save words for later.
I don't store love for "one day."
I say it. I give it. I place it.

Because I know the silence is coming.
And I want it to arrive to a heart that has nothing left to
hide.

Death isn't a thief.
It's a reminder.

It sits quietly, beside every breath,
saying:
Live while you can.
Love while you can.
And when it's time
Let go gently.

I'm not writing this to impress.
I'm writing this because it happened.
Because I saw it.

Because one day, it will be your turn to sit with death.
And I want you to know:
It's not the end.
It's just the beginning of your return.

0.11: Some Stayed.
I Saw Them.

Not everyone who entered the cancer ward left in silence.
Some walked out.
Not untouched. But alive.

I saw it with my own eyes not in stories, not on TV.
In the same halls where I watched people say goodbye,
I also saw people come back for review checkups
heads held higher, weight coming back, hair growing
again.

There were patients who had once looked too weak to
move,
now walking slowly with their families, holding new
reports.
I remember how a few nurses smiled when they saw
someone return,
months later, for a routine scan
still breathing, still fighting, still living.

No celebration.
No miracles.
Just people who kept showing up to treatment,
one day at a time.

It wasn't a dramatic recovery.
It was a decision to stay.
To keep going, even when the body was tired and the path
was uncertain.

And it mattered.
Because those who stayed reminded me
that death doesn't always win.
That survival isn't rare.
It's real.

I needed to see that.
Not to forget what I lost,
but to remember what's still possible.

Not everyone leaves.
Some remain.

And now, I've said all I needed to say.

What comes next is no longer mine.

Now, it's Death's turn to speak.
And it speaks in a voice softer than fear...
but deeper than silence.

CHAMBER

2

Sit With Me for a Moment

You don't have to be ready.
Just willing.

This is not a book about dying.
It's a book about returning.

Not to a heaven far away,
or a philosophy you must believe,
but to something closer
a truth that's always been within you,
waiting patiently.

You were taught to fear me
to run when I enter a room,
to cry when I arrive,
to whisper my name in hospitals and ceremonies
but never in everyday life.

So today, I ask only this:
Sit with me.
Not with trembling,
but with curiosity.

Imagine I am not your enemy.
Not an accident. Not a punishment.
But a pattern. A pause. A placement.

The Mandala you've been living in
circle after circle, layer after layer
was never meant to be held forever.
It was meant to be completed.

And I?
I am not here to erase it.
I am here to help you return
to the quiet center.

You may cry.
You may remember.
You may soften.

That's good. That's human.

But when you're ready,
turn the page.

I'll be waiting.

Gently.
Always.

-Death

Chapter One
Iam Not What You Think

1.1 -I Don't Wear Black

You think of me in black.
Dark robes. Empty eyes. Silence like a threat.

But that's not me.
That's fear. That's culture. That's cinema.

I wear nothing. I carry nothing. I simply arrive.
I don't bring shadows.
I bring return.

I walk into your life the way night walks into evening
 -slowly, softly.
I don't crash. I don't rush. I wait.

You fear me because you see me as an ending.
But I'm just a transition.
From the outer edge of your Mandala…
back to your center.

That's the part no one told you:
Death is not destruction.
It is placement.

I come when you are ready
-not just physically, but emotionally, energetically.

When your Mandala has completed its rhythm.
When your soul has travelled every circle it needed to.

I don't wear black.
I wear whatever truth you're ready to see.

1.2 -I Don't Come to Break, I Come to Place

You think I break things.
I don't. I arrange.

Like someone sweeping a sacred space,
I clear what no longer belongs.

You built your life like a house
full of furniture, full of roles, full of people.
But some things are no longer needed.
Some moments are complete.
Some relationships are done, even if the love remains.

When I arrive,
I don't tear it down.
I return things to where they truly belong.

Your roles return to the world.
Your pain returns to rest.
Your energy returns to stillness.
Your self -to the center.

That's what the Mandala teaches.
Not how to hold forever
but how to place what was once sacred,
without clinging to what has expired.

I don't break you.
I free you from what you were never meant to carry
forever.

1.3 -Your Last Breath Isn't the End

People imagine their last breath like a cliff.
One final gasp. Then -nothing.

But it's not like that.
It's not a fall.
It's a soft release.

Your breath -the one you've ignored all your life
suddenly becomes your friend.
It slows down.
It says, "It's okay now."
And then it lets go… not in fear, but in relief.

In Mandala language, it's the outermost circle bowing out.
The breath belongs to the body.
And the body knows: it's time.

But you?
You don't stop.

You move inward.

From the breath to the feeling.
From the feeling to the witness.
From the witness to the center.

And at the center,
there is no breath, no time, no effort.

Just presence.

Your last breath isn't the end.
It's the beginning of return.

1.4 -Pain Is Not My Voice

You blame me for the pain.
But pain is not my doing.
It belongs to life.

It is life that gets messy.
That forgets boundaries.
That loves with expectation.
That breaks, and repeats.

When I come,
I don't bring pain.
I bring pause.

Pain is the storm before I arrive.
But I am the silence after it ends.

Grief screams.
But I sit quietly in the corner.
Waiting for you to look at me without flinching.

Your pain is misplaced emotion.
It's when outer-circle chaos is allowed into your center.

The Mandala says:
Let the pain move. Let it return. Let it rest.

I'm not here to hurt you.
I'm here to hold space for what hurts.

I'm not pain.
I'm peace that looks like an ending.

1.5 -I Was with You When You Were Born

You think I only come at the end.
But I was there at the start.

When you took your first breath
I was standing behind it.
Not as a shadow, but as rhythm.

Because everything that begins… will one day return.
That's not sad. That's balance.

Birth and death are not opposites.
They are partners.
They pass the same torch.

Your Mandala started when you arrived.
But its shape was already known.
Each circle -Self, Intimacy, Society -was waiting to unfold.

I am not outside your story.
I'm woven into its pattern.

You feared me because you thought I only take.
But I gave too -the gift of a timed experience.
A chance to dance inside a body, once.

Don't see me as the final page.
I was part of the first line.

1.6 -People Blame Me for What Grief Did

When someone dies, you blame me.
But I didn't take away your love.
I only returned the form.

Grief is not caused by me.
Grief is what happens when the Mandala is unbalanced.
When you try to keep someone in a circle they've already
moved out of.

They were in your daily life.
Then I moved them to your memory.
But you try to pull them back.
That's grief.

I understand.
Love is strong.
But love doesn't need to cling.

The Mandala teaches this:
Let the energy move.
Let the bond shift from form to essence.
Let the center hold what the edges cannot.

I didn't cause the ache.
I simply revealed what was never permanent.

It hurts.
But it's not punishment.
It's placement

1.7 -The Body Is Not You. It's Your Jacket.

You spent your whole life thinking this body is you.

You looked in the mirror and said, "That's me."
But it wasn't.
It was your jacket.
And I'm just the one reminding you: time to take it off.

It was a good jacket.
It moved. It hugged. It danced. It aged.

But now, it's tired.
The cells are ready.
The breath has slowed.

You're not leaving yourself.
You're leaving the outermost circle.
Returning inward.

The Self is untouched.
It watched the body grow.
It will watch it go.

I am not the thief.
I am the tailor, saying:
"You can set this garment down now."

1.8 -I'm Not Far. I'm Always Around, Quietly.

You think I arrive suddenly.
But I've always been near.

In the sunset.
In the goodbye hugs.
In the smell of old photographs.

Not to scare.
Just to remind.

Life is precious because of me.
You feel urgency because I exist.
You love more deeply knowing it won't last forever.

Your Mandala isn't a fortress.
It's a dance of circles.
And I sit just outside -watching, smiling, silent.

Not waiting to take.
Just ready to guide.

You don't need to fear my nearness.
You've always lived with me.
You just forgot I was here.

I've always been a whisper behind your heartbeat.
Not a curse.
Just a clock.

1.9 -I Wait for the Right Time.
Never Early. Never Late.

You say, "They went too soon."
Or, "Why didn't I go yet?"

But I don't operate on human clocks.
I move by Mandala Clock.

Each soul has a pattern

Like a song,
Like a circle.
And I only step in when the pattern completes.

Not a second early.
Not a breath late.

You may not understand.
But the soul does.

Some leave young because they came to stir something,
Not to stay.
Some stay long because they're still holding light for others.

There is no mistake.
There is only timing.

Not human timing.
Sacred timing.

1.10 -I Am Not the End. I Am the Bridge.

You see a line.
Life here. Death there.
But I'm not a wall.
I'm a bridge.

I don't block the way.
I show you the way home.

You lived outside -in relationships, roles, plans.
But the Mandala always called you inward.

And when I arrive, I walk you across.
From outer identity to inner being.
From noise to stillness.

It doesn't hurt.
It doesn't confuse.
It simply returns.

I am not the end.
I am the space between what you were
and what you've always been.

Don't fear the bridge.
You've been walking toward it your whole life.

I like this one only-
remind again and continue..Now… you'll just cross it.

Chapter 2
What You Call Loss, I Call Return

2.1 -You Didn't Lose Them.
They Just Stepped Inward.

You say, "I lost them."
But they're not lost.
They just stepped inward.

You were standing in the outer circles
where bodies move, voices speak, habits live.

But they have gone closer to the center.
They haven't vanished. They've become quieter.

You search for their face, their laugh, their smell.
But now, they speak through silence.

You remember them in a photo.
They remember you through love.

They didn't disappear.
They dissolved into something truer.

You were used to reaching out.
Now you must reach in.

This is not disconnection.
It is a different kind of closeness.

What you call loss
is just someone stepping into the very deep center of their
Mandala-and waiting for you to meet them there.

2.2 -You Only Lose What You Try to Hold Too Tight

Everything you try to grip will one day slip.
Not because it was cruel -but because it was moving.

Love moves.
So does life.
So do people.

The more tightly you hold, the more afraid you become.
Because deep down, you know… everything changes.

But that's not a threat.
It's a rhythm.

When someone dies, it feels like they were taken.
But most often, they simply let go
gently, with grace.

They weren't yours to keep.
They were yours to love.

And love doesn't need to grip.
It just needs to flow.

Let them flow back to the center.
That's not losing.
That's returning.

2.3 - The Relationship Didn't End.
Only the Form Did.

You think the relationship died.
But relationships don't end.
They just change form.

What used to be presence becomes memory.
What used to be words becomes silence.
What used to be touch becomes energy.

They no longer walk beside you.
But they now walk within you.

You still hear their voice when you need it.
You still feel their strength when you are weak.

That's not imagination.
That's resonance.
That's what remains when form fades.

You miss the body.
But the bond? It's still whole.
It has simply moved closer to your heart's center.

2.4 -Love Doesn't Die.
It Just Becomes Quieter.

Love is not buried with the body.
It has no weight.
No age.
No expiry.

When someone dies, their body stops.
But their love doesn't.

It becomes quieter.
Subtler.
Deeper.

It doesn't hold your hand anymore.
It holds your decisions.

It doesn't speak aloud.
It becomes your inner voice.

You thought love meant constant presence.
But love is presence that survives absence.

They're not gone.
They're just silent now.
And sometimes, silence says the most.

2.5 -They Still Visit You.
But You Must Learn a New Language.

They're still here.
But not in the ways you expect.

They don't knock on your door.
They knock inside your thoughts.

They don't say "I'm proud of you."
But you feel their warmth when you stand tall.

They don't say "Don't cry."
But you hear them when the room goes still.

You must learn a new language.
The language of presence without form.

The Mandala doesn't close when someone dies.
It just turns inward.
You're still in it with them.

But to see them now,
you have to stop looking out
and start feeling in.

2.6 -Death Doesn't Separate.
It Repositions.

You think death takes people away.
But I don't take.
I rearrange.

The ones you love are not removed.
They're moved.

From the chair at your dinner table
to the strength in your spine.

From words in your ear
to courage in your choices.

They haven't gone.
They've gone deeper.

In Mandala language,
they've moved from the outer ring to the sacred center.

They're harder to touch,
but easier to carry.

2.7 -You'll See Them Again.
But Not with These Eyes.

You will meet them again.
Not in the way you expect.

Not in hospitals or dreams.
But in stillness.
In clarity.
In truth.

These eyes of yours
they see faces, shapes, distance.

But the heart sees differently.

One day, maybe in a breath of meditation,
or at the edge of sleep,
or in a moment of deep love
you'll see them again.

Not with your eyes,
but with your whole being.

That meeting will need no words.
Just knowing.

It will feel like peace.
Because that's where they are.

Waiting..Not far. Just deeper in.

2.8 -They Are Not Gone.
They Are Placed.

There is a difference between gone and placed.

Gone means lost.
Scattered.
Erased.

Placed means returned.
Respected.
Held.

When someone dies, they are not thrown into nothing.
They are returned to where they belong
their soul's rightful place in the larger pattern.

You miss them because they were part of your pattern too.
But the Mandala is still whole.

They are now a still point at its center,
And you are walking toward it every day.

You didn't lose them.
You'll find them at the core.

2.9 -Letting Go Isn't Forgetting.
It's Trusting.

You're afraid that letting go means forgetting.

It doesn't.

Letting go just means trusting the Mandala.
Trusting that love knows where to go.

When you hold on too tightly, you freeze love.
You stop it from moving.

But when you let go
gently, with love
you allow it to take its true shape.

Memory becomes prayer.
Sadness becomes strength.

You don't forget.
You transform.

Letting go isn't saying goodbye.
It's saying:
"I trust where you're going.
And I trust where I'm staying.
For now."

2.10 -What You Called Loss
Was Just the Door Opening

You thought it was the end.
A loss.
A break.
A door slamming shut.

But now you see -it was a door opening.

Not to absence, but to essence.

They left the surface, yes.
But they entered the heart of everything.

You didn't lose.
You gained a new way of seeing.
A new way of loving.

They became a part of stillness,
of memory,
of your next breath.

The Mandala always returns what matters.
It never ends anything without giving something deeper.

And what you called loss…
was just the opening.
Of everything.

Chapter 3
You Were Never Afraid of Death

3.1 -You Were Never Afraid of Death.
You Were Afraid of Missing Life.

You say you fear death.
But look closer.

You fear the unread books.
The unsaid words.
The undone dreams.

You fear leaving the story halfway.

You don't fear being gone.
You fear not having been here enough.

That's not fear of death.
That's fear of not living completely.

The Mandala teaches:
Live each circle fully.
Place every moment where it belongs.
Then, when the time comes,
you won't feel incomplete.

You'll feel ready.
Not because you had more time,
but because you used the time you had
with honesty.

3.2 -You Kept Waiting for the Right Time.

You kept postponing.
"I'll rest later."
"I'll say it tomorrow."
"I'll live after I've earned it."

But later doesn't always come.

Time isn't a promise.
It's a gift.

And most people waste it waiting for the perfect moment.

The perfect moment doesn't exist.
Presence does.
Now does.

The Mandala is made in the present
not in plans.

You feared death
because you thought it would steal something.

But it only steals what you never touched
the love you delayed,
the joy you postponed.

Live now.
Before now becomes memory.

3.3 -You Thought You Were Your Roles

You called yourself a teacher, a son, a wife, a leader.

But those were roles
not you.

You wore them like clothes.
Sometimes proudly.
Sometimes painfully.

But then death comes,
and gently says,
"You can take those off now."

You are not what you did.
You are what you are
when there's nothing left to prove.

The Mandala shows you this:
The outer circles are titles.
The inner circle is truth.

And truth was always quiet.
Always watching.
Always you.

You feared losing the role,
because you forgot the real one wearing it.

3.4 -You Carried So Much You Didn't Need

You carried guilt like a badge.
Carried anger like a sword.
Carried memories like they were bricks.

But you didn't have to.

So much of what burdened you
was never meant to be kept.

It stayed because you fed it.
It grew because you didn't place it.

The Mandala isn't for storage.
It's for flow.

Grief. Pain. Regret.
They move when you move.

You feared death
because your load was heavy.

But death isn't weight.
It's release.

Start now.
Lay it down.

You'll walk lighter in life, and beyond it

3.5 - You Wanted to Be Seen More Than You Wanted to Be Free

You kept trying to prove something.
To be liked. To be right.
To be important.

But being seen is not the same as being free.

You chased validation.
But it made you more afraid
afraid of failing, falling, fading.

The more eyes on you,
the less peace inside you.

You feared death
because you thought it would erase your image.

But death doesn't care about image.

It cares about essence.
And the Mandala was never impressed by noise.

It only ever waited for truth.
And truth never needs a spotlight.

3.6 -You Thought Being Busy Meant Being Alive

You filled every hour.
Meetings. Messages. Goals. Screens.

You called it ambition.
But it was noise.

Being busy doesn't mean being alive.

Presence does.

When your body stops moving,
you'll finally hear the silence.

And you'll wonder why you feared it.

The Mandala doesn't reward speed.
It honors stillness.

You were scared of death
because it looked like stopping.

But stopping is not dying.
It's remembering.

Remember now.
Before silence finds you.

3.7 -You Forgot to Breathe While You Were Breathing

Your breath was with you every second.

And yet, you forgot it.
Rushed it.
Choked it with tension.

You were alive
but barely breathing.

Your breath wasn't just air.
It was your anchor.
Your friend.
Your reminder.

In your final moment,
your breath will return to its source
not as loss,
but as surrender.

You fear that moment
because you never honored the ones before it.

The Mandala begins and ends with breath.
Each one is a circle.
Each one is enough.

Breathe now.
Feel now.

Life is here.
In this inhale.
And this release.

3.8 -You Lived as If You'd Always Have Time

You treated time like it was unlimited.

So you waited.
And waited. And waited.

You kept love on hold.
Kept healing on pause.
Kept truth for "later."

But death doesn't wait.

Not because it's cruel
because it's honest.

Time isn't forever.
It's a rhythm.

Each circle ends.
So another can begin.

You feared death
because you lived like it wouldn't come.

But when you live like time is precious,
death no longer feels like theft.

It feels like a gentle closing.
Of a door you chose to walk through with peace.

3.9 - You Were Afraid of Letting Go Before You Knew What Was Next

You wanted guarantees.
A map. A reason. A promise.

You wanted to know what comes after death
before letting go of what's now.

But that's not how truth works.

You let go first.
Then you see.

You feared death
because it asked for trust
before it gave you answers.

But trust is what grows the Mandala.
It turns the page.
It opens the door.

You were never meant to know everything.

You were meant to surrender
to something deeper than knowing.

That's not foolishness.
That's faith.
That's freedom.

3.10 -What You Called Fear
Was Just the Call to Return

That tightness in your chest?
That racing heart?
That dread at night?

That wasn't fear of death.
It was a call. A whisper.

"Come back," it said.
"To center. To presence. To peace."

You thought it was panic.
It was a longing.

Not to end,
but to begin again -from within.

The Mandala doesn't chase you.
It waits.
Until you're tired of outer noise
and ready to come home.

You called it fear.
But it was the beginning of honesty.

The return has already started.
And you don't need to run.
You just need to stop and remember.

Chapter 4
The Inner Journey
Traveling Through the Mandala of Death

4.1 -You Leave the Outermost Circle First

You begin where everyone begins -at the surface.

When death arrives, this is the first to go:
your body, your name, your voice, your plans.

This outer circle is where you lived your routine
brushing teeth, checking phones, answering emails.

It's where the noise was loudest.
Where you played roles.

When this circle drops away, it doesn't hurt.
It simply fades -like a costume being taken off.

You don't miss it the way you thought you would.
You feel relief.
Lightness.

What you once thought was you
now looks like clothing you've outgrown.

You are still here
just no longer outside.

You've stepped inward.
And the journey has just begun.

4.2 -You Say Goodbye to the Social Self

This is the circle of your face in the world
your status, your job, your reputation.

All the masks you wore so well.

Death removes them gently.

Not to shame you.
To free you.

You realize how much of your life
was built for others' eyes.

How many dreams weren't yours.
How many fears weren't real.

As this layer dissolves,
you don't lose dignity
you gain truth.

You begin to remember:
You are not what people said.
You are not what they expected.

You are something quieter,
more ancient,
more real.

This is not erasing.
This is revealing.

4.3 -The Intimate Circle Begins to Soften

Here is where your closest ties live
family, friends, lovers, children.

The people who shared your meals,
your secrets, your grief.

This layer doesn't fall away easily.

Love clings.
Memory lingers.
Faces flash.

But even here, death is gentle.

You don't forget them.
You carry them.

Their laughter echoes.
Their touch remains in you.

But the grip loosens.

Not from loss
from trust.

You begin to see that love doesn't need holding.
It just needs placement.

You no longer stand beside them.
You stand within them .Closer than ever before.

4.4 - The Circle of Identity Grows Transparent

This is where "I" lived.
Your ideas about yourself.

The good. The bad. The proud. The ashamed.

"I'm a kind person."
"I'm a failure."
"I'm important."
"I'm not enough."

All these labels… start to blur.

You don't need them here.
They served their purpose.

Now, you feel lighter
not because you have answers,
but because you have space.

You begin to ask:
If I am not the thoughts I had…
who am I?

And the question itself opens something.

This is the layer where the "I" begins to bow.

So the witness can rise.

4.5 -Emotions Return to Silence

Grief.
Guilt.
Joy.
Anger.
Hope.
Regret.

All of them lived in this circle.
They danced in your chest.
They shaped your days.

Now, as you move inward, they start to rest.

They're not denied.
They're just done.

Like guests who stayed long,
and now thank you and leave.

You don't fight them anymore.
You bless them.
And let them go.

Your heart feels open,
but not flooded.

The Mandala allows emotion.
But not forever.

They taught you.
They stretched you.
But they are not you.

And now…
you are ready for quiet.

4.6 -The Mind Finally Slows Down

Thoughts don't stop all at once.
They float.
They rewind.
They visit.

But they don't control you now.

You are no longer the thinker.
You are the space around thought.

You used to believe your mind was everything.

Now, it's like background music in another room.

The more you move inward,
the more silence grows.

And that silence feels rich not empty.

This is where the Mandala becomes wide and still.

Not because you lost something.
But because you've returned to what was always steady.

You're not forgetting.
You're remembering.

Who you were before the thinking began.

4.7 -The Breath Says Goodbye,
But the Self Stays

The final breath doesn't feel like collapse.
It feels like a bow.

The lungs exhale,
not in struggle
but in surrender.

The breath came and went a thousand times.
You forgot it every day.

But now it leaves with honor.

Like a loyal friend who stayed until the end.

And you…
you remain.

Not as a breath,
not as a body
but as being.

The Mandala's outermost movement has finished.

But what's left
is the unmoving core.
You.

Still here.Still aware..Still whole.

4.8 - You Become the Witness, Not the Story

You watched your life like a movie.
Now you step out of the screen.

You are not the character anymore.
Not the script.
Not the scene.

You are the one who watched it all unfold.

Calm. Still. Awake.

There's no applause.
No regret.

Only knowing.

This is what the Mandala was always guiding you toward:
not performance,
but presence.

You are the witness.
Pure.
Unattached.
Unshaken.

And it is beautiful
to be no one but yourself. Finally.

4.9 -You Rest in the Deepest Center of the Mandala

There is nowhere left to go.
Nothing more to become.

You have passed through every circle
from body to breath,
from roles to raw truth.

And now,
you rest in the deepest center.

It is still here.
The place that never moved.

You feel no fear.
No grief.
No rush.

Just peace.

Everything else was a wave.
This is the ocean.

Here, you don't ask questions.
Because nothing is missing.

You are home.

4.10 -The Journey Was Inward All Along

You thought death was an event.
A moment.
A fall.

But it wasn't.
It was a return.

Not out into nothing.
But in
into the truth you always carried.

Every role, every fear, every attachment
they were just circles pulling you home.

You didn't lose yourself.
You peeled back what wasn't you.

And what remained was stillness.

Awareness.

You.

The journey wasn't away.
It was in.

The Mandala never ends.
It completes.

And when it does
you don't disappear.

You dissolve
into the one who always was.

Chapter 5
The Final Return
Death as Birth

5.1 -You Thought the End Would Hurt. It Doesn't.

You were afraid of how it would feel
as if something would break, or vanish, or explode.

But none of that happens.

The end is not loud.
It's soft.
Like breath settling.
Like music pausing.

It doesn't hurt. It holds.

You are not torn apart.
You are gently gathered in.

The body lets go without fear.
The breath releases like a prayer.

You realize… it was never ending you feared.
It was resistance.

And now, there's nothing left to resist. Only rest.

5.2 -The Room Feels Like a River

You feel the room around you dissolve.
Not disappear -dissolve.

It's no longer walls and corners.
It's motion. Warmth. Flow.

You feel yourself moving,
but not forward or backward
inward.

Like a leaf on a river,
you're carried without effort.

You're not being pulled.
You're being welcomed.

Every part of you softens.

Even your questions stop asking.

And the river says,
"You're safe. You're seen. Float."

So you do.

5.3 -Your Breath Says Thank You

It's strange, but you feel it.

Your breath
the one that's been with you since the beginning
it whispers something before leaving:

"Thank you."

Not for being perfect.
Not for doing everything right.

Just… for letting it serve you.
For showing up to life, again and again.

Breath doesn't need applause.
Just presence.

And now, as it leaves,
it does not cling.
It bows.

And you bow too.

With gratitude, not fear.

This is not giving up.
This is giving back.

5.4 -You Let Go Gently.
Not With Regret.

You don't have to be dragged.

You're not screaming.
You're not begging for more.

You let go like a leaf lets go of a branch
when the wind is right.

There's no regret.
Because everything that needed to happen,
did.

Not perfectly.
But truthfully.

The letting go is not an accident.
It's grace.

This is not a fall.
It's a release.

You didn't run away.
You returned.

5.5 -Everyone You Loved Is Here.
But Not As You Knew Them

You don't see them with eyes.

But you feel them.
The ones you missed.
The ones you loved.
The ones you didn't get to say goodbye to.

They're not faces.
They're presence.

Not memories.
Essence.

You don't need names here.
You just know.

Their energy touches yours,
not in noise, but in stillness.

No more expectations.
Only recognition.

You don't cry.
You remember.

And remembering feels like peace.

5.6 -You Remember Who You Really Are

Not your name.
Not your roles.
Not your story.

You remember you.

The watcher.
The center.
The quiet self you met only in rare moments
under a tree, or at night, or in deep stillness.

Now, it's the only thing left.
And it's enough.

You are not light.
You are what light comes from.

Not a soul flying away.
A self returning inward.

You are what you were before the beginning.
And what remains after the end.

You are not a part of the Mandala.
You are its still core.

5.7 - You Feel Weightless
Not Floating, But Free

It's not like flying.
It's like not needing to.

You don't feel lifted.
You feel released.

There's nothing pulling you.
Nothing pushing you.
Just ease.

You feel free from time.
Free from form.
Free from proving anything.

It's not a rush.
It's a rest.

Weightlessness doesn't mean losing gravity.
It means you are no longer trying to hold everything together.

You were never meant to carry so much.

Now, you simply are.

And that is light enough.

5.8 -It's Not Dark. It's Quiet

People said death was dark.

But it isn't.

It's quiet.
Beautifully, richly, completely quiet.

Not the silence of emptiness.
The silence of fullness.

No clocks.
No questions.
No sound that asks for attention.

Just stillness
like a deep lake without wind.

You don't miss noise.

You remember how noise was often a cover.
Now, without it,
you feel clarity.

This isn't the dark.
This is the truth without commentary.

This is where truth speaks
without words

5.9 -You Were Never Alone

Even when you thought you were.
Even when the room was empty.
Even when the world was quiet.

You were held.

You were seen.

You were guided
by something too quiet to shout,
but too present to ignore.

Now, you feel it fully.

That presence.
That pattern.
That Mandala that never let go of you,
even when you let go of yourself.

You're not alone.
You never were.
And you never will be.

This knowing is not comforting.
It's complete.

5.10 -Now, You Are Born

You thought you died.
But you didn't.

You returned.

From noise to stillness.
From identity to essence.
From fear to peace.

What you called death
was a birth without a cry.
A beginning without a bang.

You were not erased.
You were refined.

Now, you are whole.
Now, you are new.

You are not less.
You are more than you've ever been.

This is not goodbye.
This is the deepest hello.

You are not gone.
Now, you are born.

And now...
Let the Mandala Speak.

CHAMBER

3

You've heard the witness.
You've heard Death.

But before you close this book,
you need to know one thing.

Now, it's my turn.

M.1- Why I Am Speaking Now

You've already read much.

You've seen how death came.
You've seen what it does to a body, to a family, to a mind.

You've walked through fear,
through hospital halls,
through the silence that fills a house after someone is gone.

You've asked the questions that matter:
Why did they go?
Why couldn't I stop it?
What does it all mean?

And still, something in you
has not fully rested.

Not because you are weak.
But because no one really told you the truth.
Not clearly.
Not gently.
Not in a way your heart could hear.

So I am speaking now.

Not because I have answers.
But because I have seen something
that can set you free
if you are ready to see it too.

You have carried grief like a burning coal.
You have held memories like lifelines.

You have called it love.
And it is.

But there is a kind of love
that does not hold the past tight.
It simply understands what death truly is
and makes peace with it.

That is the love I want to show you.

So let me speak now.
Not as a teacher.
Not as a saint.
But as someone who has sat where you are sitting
and seen what comes next.

Read this part slowly.
This is not more knowledge.
This is your release.

M.2- You Lost Someone. But They Didn't Leave. Let's Talk About That.

They were here.
And then they were not.

That's what your heart keeps repeating,
even if your mind has moved on.

One moment they were breathing beside you.
The next moment, it was only a body.

People say things:
"It's okay."
"They're in a better place."
"Time will heal."

But time doesn't answer the questions
you ask at night when no one is listening.

Where did they go?
Did they feel pain?
Are they really gone?
Are they somewhere?
Can they hear me?

You don't need more words.
You need someone to tell you clearly:
they didn't leave.

What left was the form.
The body.
The breath.

But what you loved about them
was never the body.
It was something that cannot be touched
and so it cannot disappear.

You didn't fall in love with their heartbeat.
You loved something deeper,
something that looked through their eyes
and reached you without needing to explain.

That thing
is not gone.

It has changed shape.
It has changed direction.

But it is not far.

You are not crazy for still feeling them.
You are not weak for still needing them.
You are simply close to a truth most people never stop to
see.

They didn't leave.
You just need to learn how to listen in a different way
now.

And I can help you with that.
If you stay with me.

M.3-The Pain Is Real.

But the Story About Death Is Not.

What you felt was real.

The shock.
The ache.
The emptiness.

No one should take that from you.
And I will not.

But what I will ask you to look at is this:

The pain is real.
But the story around it
may not be.

You were told death is the end.
That it comes to take.
That it separates.
That it steals.

You were told life is here
and death is somewhere else.
That living people are "with us"
and the dead are "gone."

But none of that is true.

You felt grief
because something beautiful shifted form
faster than your heart was ready for.

But the beauty itself
did not end.

You still carry it.
You still hear their voice in your dreams.
You still pause at their name
not because you are broken
but because something in you still knows
they are not far.

The pain is real
but the weight of it
comes from believing a lie:
that death erased them
and left you alone.

No.

Death changed the room.
Not the love.

They are still here.
And the moment you stop clinging to the old shape
you will begin to feel the truth of that.

Let the pain be there.
But do not carry the lie with it.

M.4- You Feared Their Ending.

But They Were Not What Ended.

You watched them fade.

Maybe slowly.
Maybe suddenly.
Maybe in your arms.
Maybe far away.

And something in you broke
not just because they were gone,
but because it felt like the world had ended with them.

Their voice.
Their touch.
Their place in your life.

Everything felt torn open.

But now I must tell you something that may sound strange
at first.
And I say it carefully, with love.

They did not end.

What ended was the version of them
that your eyes could see
and your hands could hold.

But what you truly knew
what you loved in them,
what felt alive behind the skin
was never the skin.

It was never the voice.
It was never the personality.
It was something else.
Something you could not name
but felt more clearly than anything else.

That part did not end.

It could not.

Because it was never made of parts.

You fear endings
because you believe form is the whole truth.

But form is only the clothing.
Only the doorway.

They walked through.
But what you loved is still walking.

Not beside you.
But within you.

Not to comfort.
But because it was always there
even before you met them.

What ended
was only the frame.

What remains
is the light that was always shining through it.

M.5- What Dies Is Never the Love.

Only the Form.

You miss them.

That's not a weakness.
That's not attachment.
That is love still warm, still alive,
still looking for a place to rest.

But listen to me now.

What you lost
was not the love.

You lost the form.
The hands.
The timing.
The laughter on certain days.

That part had to go.

Because form cannot last.
No matter how tightly you hold it.

But love
real love
the kind that doesn't depend on memory or touch
the kind that existed even when they were silent
that love is untouched by endings.

It wasn't created by their presence.
It was revealed by it.

And now that they are gone,
you think the love has nowhere to go.

But it does.

It goes deeper.
It goes inward.
It moves from your hands into your breath,
from your memory into your being.

You don't stop loving.
You **become** the love.

And in becoming it,
you realize what died
was the shape of a relationship.

What survived
is the truth beneath it.

And that truth
is still here.

Right now.
As you read this.
As you remember them.

That is why your chest aches.

Not because something ended.
But because something eternal
has nowhere left to hide.

M.6- Where Do They Go?

Let Me Show You

You've asked this quietly, again and again.

Where did they go?

Are they floating?
Watching?
Resting somewhere?

You want to know because if you could picture it
you might feel less lost.

I understand.

I used to imagine too.

But the truth is both simpler and harder than any image.

They didn't go anywhere.

They returned to where they always were
beneath the form.

They did not float upward.
They didn't travel far.

They simply stopped being separate.

When they were alive,
you saw them as a person
with a face, a voice, a name.

But what you really knew
what made you stop and love them
was never their form.

It was the quiet presence inside it.
The spark that couldn't be described
but was more real than their words.

That spark didn't go.

It was never outside you to begin with.

It is the same spark
that lives in your own stillness.
The same presence that looks out of your eyes
when you are not trying to be anyone.

They didn't move.
They **merged**.

Into what?
Into the silence behind all things.
Into the space that holds all love.

And if you ever sit quietly long enough,
you'll feel it.

Not as a ghost.
Not as memory.

But as the part of you
that has no beginning
and cannot end.

That is where they are.
And it is not far.

M.7- Why Death Had to Happen That Way

You still replay it.

How it happened.
What you could've done.
What they said.
What you didn't get to say.

Some part of you still whispers
It shouldn't have happened like that.
Not that fast.
Not that painfully.
Not that day.

And I will not argue with your heart.
Because your pain is real.

But let me say something you may not have heard before.

It did not happen by mistake.

Even if it looked unfair.
Even if it felt cruel.
Even if it shattered you.

It happened
the only way it could have
for what needed to be complete
to be complete.

You may not see it now.
You may not agree.
But one day, when you are quiet enough inside,

you will see that what left you
was also **returning something to you**.

Not a gift you wanted.
But a turning you needed.

Their leaving woke something in you.
It shook the walls.
It stopped the pretending.

You began to ask real questions.

You began to feel what matters.

You began, maybe for the first time,
to sit with silence
without fighting it.

Death happened that way
not because it was just
but because it was **true**.

And truth
always chooses the path
that takes you
to what's real.

Even if it hurts first.

M.8- You Are Not Ready to Die Yet.

But You Can Stop Fearing It.

You are still here.
Alive.
Reading this.
Breathing.

And maybe somewhere in you
there's a fear you don't speak aloud.

What if it comes suddenly?
What if I suffer?
What if I disappear?
What if no one remembers?

Even if you believe in peace after death,
some part of you holds back.

I see that.
I have felt it too.

But let me tell you something simple.

You are not ready to die yet.
Because there are things in you still calling to be seen.
Still waiting to be released.
Still longing to be touched.

That's not wrong.
That's not weakness.
That's the intelligence of life itself.

But you can stop fearing death
by stopping the war with it.

You don't need to chase it.
You don't need to deny it.

You only need to understand
that death doesn't come to erase you.
It comes to **complete** what has already begun.

And right now, you are still in the middle of that
becoming.

So live.
Fully.
Softly.
Consciously.

And when the moment comes
not now,
but one day
you will not run from it.

You will recognize it.
Like an old friend
who has always waited quietly
outside your door.

And you will not say goodbye.
You will say
Thank you. I'm ready.

M.9- Nothing Was Taken from You.

It Was Given Back to Where It Belonged.

You still feel like something was stolen.

Like death came into your life
and ripped out something sacred.
Like it walked away with your joy,
your closeness,
your future.

You wake up some days
and feel the absence like a weight on your chest.

And I won't pretend it doesn't hurt.
I won't say you should feel differently.

But I will ask you to look again.

Not with the eyes of fear.
But with the eyes of truth.

Because nothing was stolen.
Not really.

What you loved was not taken from you.
It was returned
to the source it came from.

Not far away.
Not out of reach.
But into a space

that does not depend on breath
or time
or form.

You did not lose them.
You carried them
as long as they could stay.
And when it was time,
life gently let go of what it could no longer hold.

That is not robbery.
That is release.

It doesn't mean you don't ache.
It doesn't mean you don't miss them.

It just means you can stop fighting the river
and start trusting the flow.

What belonged to this world
served its time.

What was beyond this world
has gone home.

And one day,

so will you.

M.10- If They Could Speak to You Now, They Would Say This

I know you still wonder
what they would say
if they had one more moment.
One more breath.
One more chance to speak to you
before they slipped from this world.

You've imagined it.

Sometimes at night,
sometimes in dreams,
sometimes in the quiet moments no one else sees.

Let me say to you
what they could not say
but what they have always wanted you to know.

They would say:

"I didn't leave you.
I only stopped being where you could see me.
But I never stopped being near.

You don't need to keep grieving like you failed me.
You didn't.
You gave me more love than you know.

You don't need to hold onto the guilt.
You were there.

Even when you weren't near,
your love never left me.

And now I am not far.

I have no voice now
but I live in the way your chest warms
when you remember my smile.

I have no eyes
but I see through your tears
when you say my name softly.

You don't have to move on.
Just move inward.
I am not gone.
I am just quiet now.

Live your life.
Not in spite of me.
But for me.

And one day,
when you come close,
you will not need to ask if I'm there.

You will already know."

M.11- What Remains After Everything Is Gone

By now, you've let go of much.

People.
Expectations.
Certainty.
Moments that once felt permanent.

You've seen how things fall away.
Sometimes gently.
Sometimes violently.
Sometimes all at once.

You've seen how nothing you love
can stay exactly the way it was.

And it hurts.

But I want you to pause with me now
and look closely.

After all the endings…
after the departures,
the silence,
the grief…

what is still here?

Look beyond your memories.
Beneath your sorrow.
Under your breathing.

What remains?

Not the form.
Not the voice.
Not the idea of who you are.

But something that doesn't need words.
Something that didn't begin,
so it doesn't end.

It doesn't speak.
But it knows.

It doesn't change.
But it holds everything that does.

That is what remains
when everything else has gone.

Not an answer.
Not a belief.
But a presence.

It was here before your first goodbye.
It will be here after your last breath.

You don't need to chase it.
You just need to stop calling it something else.

It is not a person.
It is not a soul.
It is not a voice in the sky.

It is what loved through you.
And what you will return to
when there's nothing left to carry.

M.12- Let This Be the Last Thing You Need to Hear About Death

You have carried these pages through many rooms inside you.
You have remembered.
You have cried.
You have softened.
You have let go not of them, but of the weight.

And now you are here.

You don't need another explanation.
You don't need more meaning.
You don't need to believe anything new.

You only need this one truth.
And once you feel it,
you won't need anything after it.

Here it is:

Nothing has truly ended.

What you saw as death
was not a shutting down.
It was a **placing**.
A returning.
A dissolving of form back into what was always formless.

And what remains is not an echo.
Not a memory.
Not even love.

What remains is..

what was always there before anyone arrived.

The stillness you ignored.
The space between breaths.
The presence that held you even before your name had
meaning.

You are not being asked to understand this.
You are being asked to rest in it.

Close the book.
Let the stories be stories.
Let the losses be sacred.
Let the silence finish what these words began.

You are not alone.
You are not ending.
You are not holding anything broken.

You are home.
You always were.
And now you remember.

That is all.

You came looking for answers.
You found a mirror.
You listened for something that would make it all make sense.

But now there is no more to listen to.

What you lost
was never truly lost.

What you feared
was never truly separate.

What you are
does not need to be saved.

And what comes next
is not death.

It is the part of you
that was never touched by time
finally becoming all that remains.

So put this book down.
Not like you finished it.

Put it down
like a story that's no longer needed.

Let the silence close around you.

Let what is true
become the only thing still breathing.

And let that be enough. Forever.

Take Care now,
Mandala will meet you again.